Solar System Explorers

Mars

Written by
E.C. Andrews

KidHaven
PUBLISHING

Published in 2026 by
KidHaven Publishing, an Imprint of
Greenhaven Publishing, LLC
2544 Clinton St., Buffalo, NY 14224

Written by: E.C. Andrews
Edited by: Noah Leatherland
Designed by: Amelia Harris

Cataloging-in-Publication Data
Names: Andrews, E.C.
Title: Mars / E.C. Andrews.
Description: Buffalo, NY : Kidhaven Publishing, 2026. | Series: Solar System Explorers | Includes glossary and index
Identifiers: ISBN 9781534549791 (pbk) | ISBN 9781534549807 (library bound) | ISBN 9781534549814 (ebook)
Subjects: LCSH: Mars (Planet)—Juvenile Literature
Classification: LCC QB641 A53 2026 | DDC 523.43--dc25

Manufactured in the United States of America

CPSIA compliance information: Batch #CSKH26
For further information contact Greenhaven Publishing LLC at 1-844-317-7404.

Please visit our website, www.greenhavenpublishing.com.
For a free color catalog of all our high-quality books, call toll free 1-844-317-7404 or fax 1-844-317-7405.

Find us on

Image Credits

Images are courtesy of Shutterstock.com. With thanks to Getty Images, Thinkstock Photo and iStockphoto. Cover – Pike-28, AspctStyle, andreysharonov, Artsiom P. Recurring Images – thomas eder, YummyBuum, Sabelskaya. 4-5 – Artsiom P, Joseph Jacobs. 6-7 – bilgeari, Alones. 8-9 – Juergen Faelchle, Andrey Yurlov. 10-11 – AspctStyle. 12-13 – Moonnoon, Artsiom P, Vadim Sadovski. 14-15 – ConceptCafe, Nazarii_Neshcherenskyi. 16-17 – Vlad Ra27, Evgeniyqw, Artsiom P. 18-19 – AspctStyle, Dima Zel, Vadim Sadovski, Claudio Caridi. 20-21 – ConceptCafe, Nazarii_Neshcherenskyi, Artsiom P, itechno. 22-23 – Aphelleon.

Contents

Words that look like this can be found in the glossary on page 24.

Let's Explore!

The solar system is a group of planets and other objects that orbit a star. This star is called the sun. Have you ever wanted to explore the solar system?

Exploring the solar system is a big adventure, but we explorers are up for the challenge. So, hop aboard our spaceship and discover the solar system with us.

Where Is Mars?

Every planet in the solar system orbits the sun at a different distance. If we were to line them up in order, it would look something like this:

Mars is the fourth planet. It is in between Earth and Jupiter. Mars is about 142 million miles (228 million km) from the sun. Can you count how many planets are farther away from the sun than Mars?

Round and Round

It takes Earth about 365 days to orbit the sun once. We call this a year. As Mars is farther away, it takes about 687 days to orbit the sun. That is nearly two Earth years.

As planets orbit the sun, they are also spinning on an **axis**. One full spin is called a day. An Earth day is twenty-four hours. A Mars day is around twenty-five Earth hours.

Planet Profile

Let's check the database to see what we know about Mars so far.

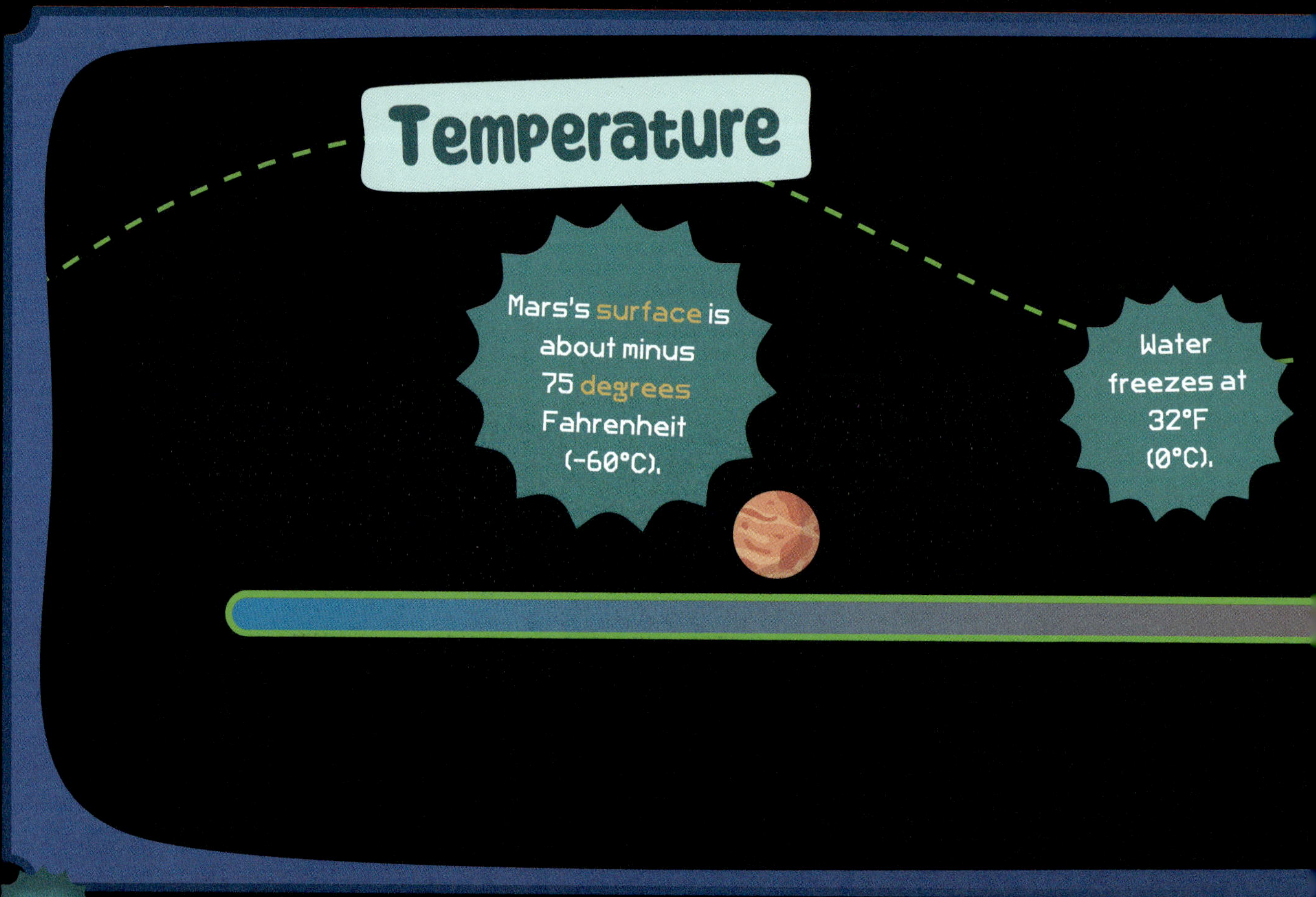

Size

- Around: 13,300 miles (21,343 km)
- Across: 4,222 miles (6,794 km)

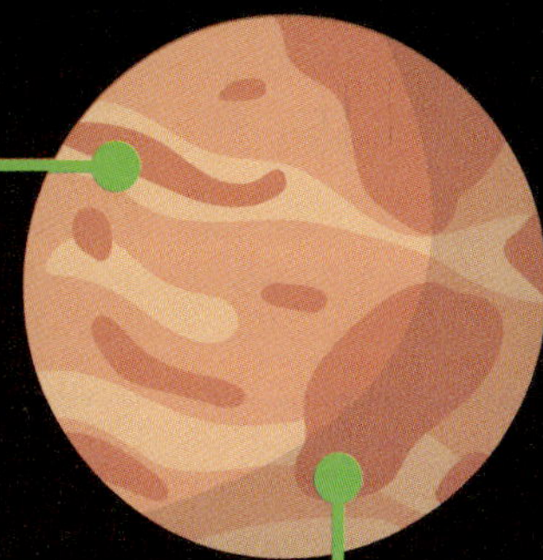

Water boils at 212°F (100° C).

What Is Mars Made Of?

Mars is a rocky planet. It has a hard surface that is made from rocks and different kinds of metals. Many rocks on Mars are full of a metal called iron.

surface of Mars

Mars is thought to have three main layers.

Crust

The crust is the planet's surface. Mars's surface is full of iron and other metals.

Mantle

Mars has a soft mantle made of **gases** and metals.

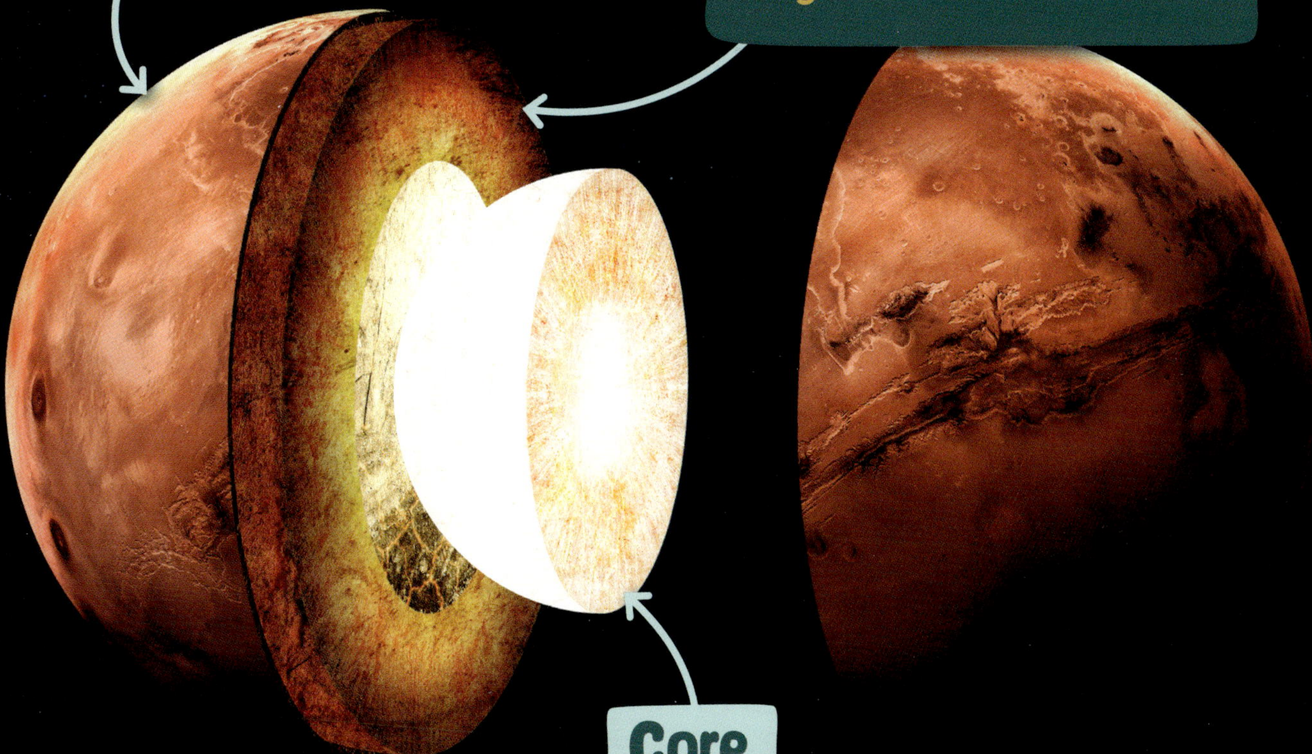

Core

The core is made of hot liquid metals, such as iron and nickel.

Watching the Weather

Mars is much colder than Earth. It is also quite windy. Mars's crust is covered in dust, so the wind causes lots of dust storms. Some dust storms can last for up to three weeks.

There is water on Mars. However, because it is so cold, most of the water is frozen. There is also water vapor in the **atmosphere**. Water vapor is water that has turned into gas.

Is There Life on Mars?

So far, we have not found life on Mars. However, it is possible that there used to be life on Mars. Scientists believe Mars used to be warmer and covered in water.

A planet that living things can survive on is called habitable.

Some scientists think Mars might be habitable in the future. This means humans may be able to live on Mars. However, this is not known for certain yet.

Something that orbits around a bigger object in space is called a satellite. Some satellites are **natural**. A moon is a natural satellite. However, some satellites are made by humans.

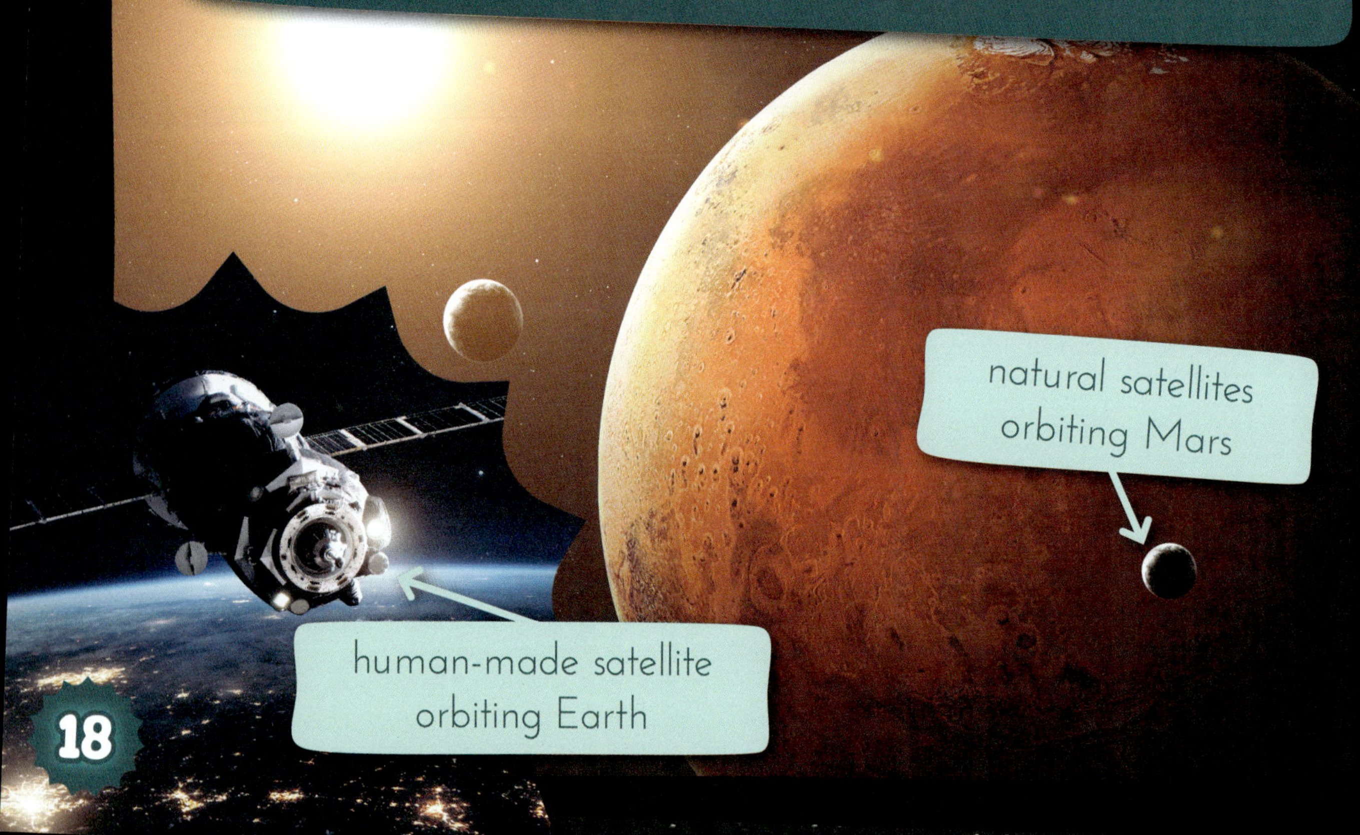

Mars has two moons. They are called Phobos and Deimos. They are the smallest moons in the solar system. Phobos orbits closer to its planet than any other moon in the solar system.

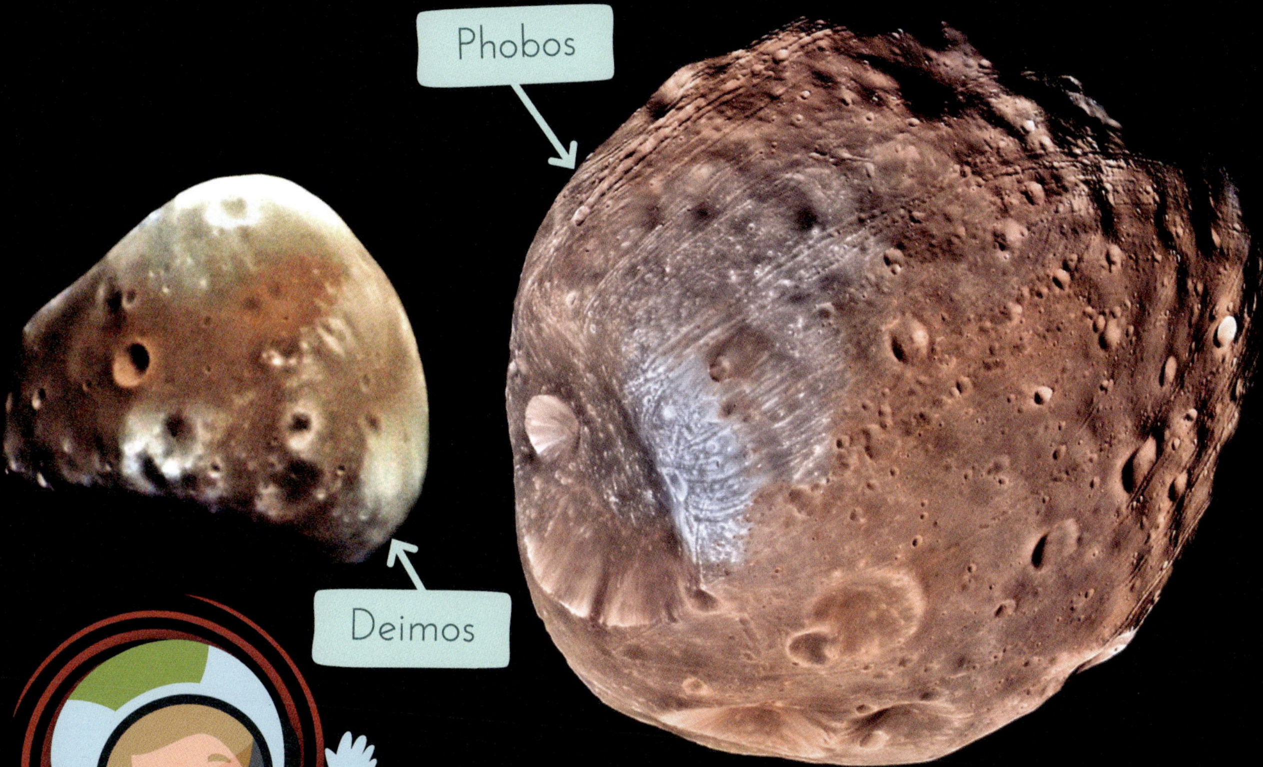

The Red Planet

Some scientists call Mars "the Red Planet." Mars is red because of the iron in the rocks. When iron touches air, it goes red. Iron is also one of the things that makes blood red.

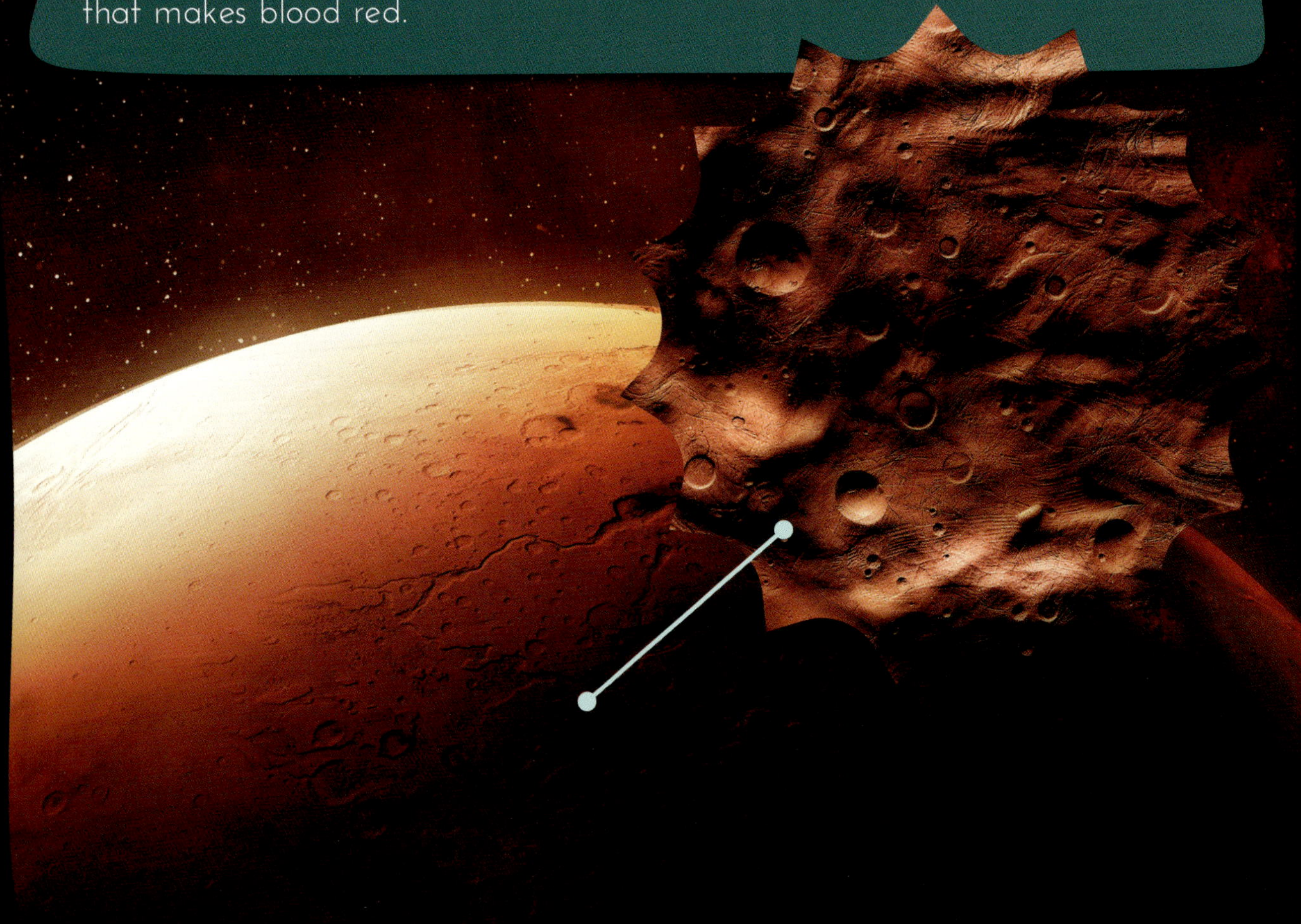

Mars was named by the **ancient** Romans. They named the planet after their god of war. This is because they thought the planet's red color looked like blood.

the ancient Roman god, Mars

More to Explore

We have had a magnificent time on Mars. We have gathered lots of new information to add to our database. What was the most fascinating thing you learned?

It is now time to wave goodbye to the Red Planet. The solar system is a very big place and there is still much more to explore.

Glossary

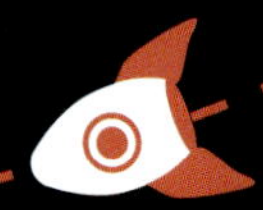

ancient	belonging to the very distant past
atmosphere	the mixture of gases that makes up the air and surrounds a planet
axis	an imaginary line that something turns on
degree	a measuring unit used to explain how hot or cold something is
gases	things that are like air, which fill any space available
natural	found in nature and not made by people
orbit	move around a star or planet in a curved path
surface	the outside layer of something
survive	to stay alive

Index